CHECKLISTS FOR NORMAL DEVELOPMENT 0-5

A quick and easy guide.

By Alice Hare, Paediatric Occupational Therapist.

Table of Contents

ABOUT THE AUTHOR

Alice Hare studied at the University of Queensland, in Australia, graduating with a Bachelor of Occupational Therapy in 1979. She also studied psychology at the same university. Her first job in the early 1980s was with the Cerebral Palsy League (Australia), working with children with disabilities including CP, spina bifida, and visual impairment.

From this early start, she moved into Government working for Queensland Health in the Developmental Assessment Team (DAT). Here she discovered she had a natural affinity with children of all ages. Kids liked her.

Whilst at DAT Alice refined her skills in the use of formal assessment tools to determine areas of delay in children. She worked closely with families, other health professionals and teachers to assist children to reach their full potential. It was here that she began her work in the development of children's self-esteem. She also ran Social Skills groups, primarily for kids with features of autism, with exceptional results. Alice designed and ran Parent Education groups as well as training child care workers in child development and basic developmental screening.

Alice is an accredited trainer in Triple P, a parent education program to upskill parents in child behaviour management. She is also an accredited trainer in play therapy, running "Learn to Play" workshops for early childhood teachers, and child health workers.

Alice has also worked for Education Queensland, focussing on assisting children with enuresis and encopresis (poor control of wees and poos).

At Child Health, in her last paediatric position, Alice became accredited in Sand Play therapy.

She worked with many children with learning difficulties, as well as those with neurological atypical development and sensory issues including children with ASD and ADHD. A large part of Alice's role was to assess children in consultation with families, carers and teachers, and refer, as required, to other members of the multi-disciplinary team and to the Paediatrician for formal diagnosis.

INTRODUCTION

One of the greatest pleasures a parent has is to watch their child grow and progress. Every parent is excited when their baby says her first word,or, takes his first steps alone.

This is the reason that I wrote this book. Using this little book as a guide, as their child grows, parents can understand what they are seeing unfold, and fully enjoy the anticipation of knowing what comes next.

Parents will tell you that all children are different, and this is true. There are many factors that influence children's development, including the child's temperament, health and sense of security. Undoubtedly a stable environment where a child feels safe and loved is most conducive to the child reaching their full potential. The richness of a child's environment impacts on development also.

Even taking all these variables into account, we can still predict what a child should be doing within a certain age range. There is a pattern to the progress that all normal children will follow, in their own time.

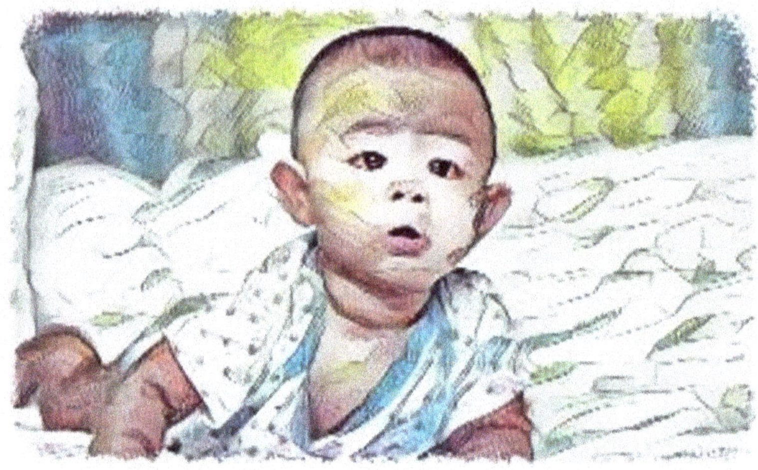

WHY AWARENESS OF CHILD DEVELOPMENT IS IMPORTANT.

Being aware of this natural progression and the average range for developmental skills allows parents to check if their child is basically on track.

Having access to a developmental checklist enables concerned parents to monitor their own child's development at home. Parents will be empowered to recognise if their child is falling too far behind. Early recognition of significant delays allows parents to seek advice from professionals in child health and development who can advise and support them.

It is now well understood that early intervention for children with delays is the ideal way of ensuring they get the best start in life. Early intervention at the youngest possible age, allows the child to catch up and be the best they can be.

SCHOOL READINESS

In addition, the milestones at 4 and 5 years in the following checklists, will give parents vital information on their child's readiness for school. Parents can then have confidence that their child will cope with the demands of formal schooling.

6 months

6 months

Movement milestones -

held sitting

- Sits with support in pram or highchair

- On his back lifts legs and grabs one foot

- In sitting, head is held upright

- Rolls over

- When held standing puts weight through legs

- Placed on tummy, pushes up on arms.

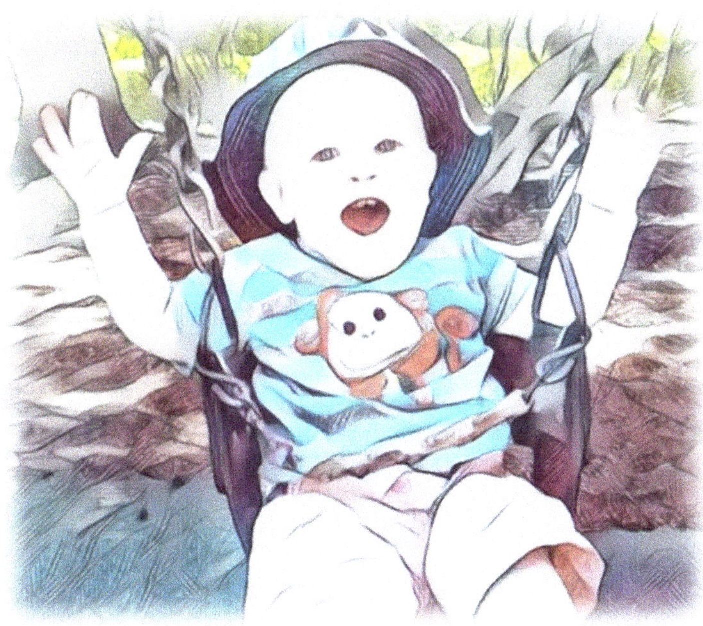

6 months
Vision and hand skills -

swaps hands

- Watches movements around room
- Grasps with whole hand
- Swaps items hand to hand
- Watches where toy falls
- Grasps and plays with own feet

6 months
Hearing and speech -
laughs

- Turns to parent's voice
- Laughs and squeals in play
- Babbles to self.

6 months
Social behaviour and play -
mouths everything

- Grasps rattle and shakes

- Puts hands on feeding bottle

- Takes everything to mouth

Tracking my child's journey

Name: Date:

Age:

Big movements:

Hand movements:

This page is for you to write on.

Speech and understanding:

Social behaviour and play:

Comments (e.g. illnesses):

12 months

12 months

Movement milestones

Stands, may walk.

- Walks holding on to furniture
- Gets to sitting position without assistance
- Assumes hands-and-knees position
- Crawls (on belly) or hands and knees
- Gets from sitting to crawling or prone (lying on stomach) position
- Pulls self up on furniture to stand
- Stands momentarily without support
- May walk two or three steps without support

12 months

Milestones in hand & finger skills
points

- Uses thumb to index finger grasp (pincer grasp)

- Bangs two cubes together
- Puts objects into container
- Takes objects out of container
- Lets objects go voluntarily
- Pokes and points with index finger
- Tries to imitate scribbling

12 months

Speech -

one word

- Responds to simple verbal requests
- Says "dada" and "mama"
- Babbles loudly.
- Tries to imitate words (ecolalia)
- Beginning to show interest in pictures
- Understands several words in context (cup, ball)

21

- Understands simple instruction with gesture (e.g. wave bye-bye).

12 months

Behaviour and play –

drinks from cup

- Chews food

- Starting to drink from cup

- Puts objects into and out of containers

- Likes to be able to see and hear familiar adults

- Claps hands

- Sits without support to be dressed

This page is for you to write on.
Tracking my child's journey

Name: Date:

Age:

Big movements:

Hand movements:

Speech and understanding:

Social behaviour and play:

Comments (e.g. illnesses):

18 months

18 months
Movement milestones

walks well

- Walks well
- Runs carefully
- Pushes and pulls large toys
- Starting to climb onto furniture
- Walks up stairs with help.
- Climbs downstairs on tummy or forward on bottom

18 months
Milestones in hand & finger skills

holds pencil

- Holds pencil and scribbles

- Stacks 3 blocks after demonstration
- Starting to prefer one hand
- Enjoys simple picture books
- Turns pages several at a time.

18 months

Speech -

uses some words

- Uses 6 to 20 words and understands many more
- Tries to join in nursery rhymes
- Gives familiar objects to parent when asked
- Follows very simple instructions e.g. "shut the door"
- Shows own nose, feet and hair (and often on doll)

18 months
Behaviour and play –

chews well

- Chews well
- Drinks with little spilling from cup
- Can remove own shoes, socks and hat
- Beginning to predict own wees and poos.
- Usually has stopped putting everything to mouth
- Remembering where objects belong
- Plays alone but near familiar adults
- Enjoys putting objects into containers
- Emotionally still very dependent on carer (especially mother)

Tracking my child's journey

Name: Date:

Age:

Big movements:

Hand movements:

Speech and understanding:

Social behaviour and play:

Comments (e.g. illnesses):

2 years

2 years

Movement milestones –

runs well

- Pushes small tricycle but can't use pedals

- Runs well

- Squats

- Tries to kick a ball

- Climbs onto and down from furniture unassisted

- Walks up and down stairs holding on to support

- Throws small ball overhand

2 years
Milestones in hand and finger skills -

holds pencil, scribbles

- Holds pencil and scribbles spontaneously
- Imitates drawing vertical line
- Might use one hand more frequently than the other
- Spoon feeds self without spilling
- Uses cup, usually without spilling
- Turns over container to pour out contents
- Builds tower of 6 or 7 blocks
- Enjoys picture books and turns single pages

2 years

Language milestones –

2-4 word sentences

- Uses 50 or more recognizable words (understands more)

- Listens to others talking
- Uses two to four-word sentences
- Points to object or picture when it's named
- Uses own name
- Recognizes names of familiar people, objects, and body parts
- Joins in nursery rhymes and songs
- Follows simple instructions e.g. "give to Daddy"
- Repeats words overheard in conversation

2 years
Play and behaviour –

plays near but not with other children

- Plays near but not with other children (parallel play)
- Asks for food and drink
- Puts on hat and shoes
- Beginning to predict when needing to wee and poo
- Often dry through the night

- Turns door handles (not aware of dangers)
- Simple pretend play
- Copies household tasks in play
- Clings tightly when frightened
- Tantrums when frustrated
- Not good at sharing toys or adult's attention
- Begins to sort/match shapes and colors
- No understanding of need to wait for things
- pretend plays with doll/car

This page is for you to write on.

Tracking my child's journey

Name: Date:

Age:

Big movements:

Hand movements:

Speech and understanding:

Social behaviour and play:

Comments (e.g. illnesses):

3 years

3 years
Movement milestones -

rides trike using pedals

- Walks alone up and down steps
- Kicks ball forcibly
- Jumps two feet together
- Climbs well
- Can walk backwards and sideways
- Rides tricycle using pedals
- Can throw and catch a large ball between extended arms

3 years
Milestones in hand skills -

draws circle and cross

- Stacks 9 blocks
- Threads large beads

- Holds pencil in preferred hand with good control
- Draws a circle, and copies cross and some letters
- Eats with fork and spoon
- Enjoys painting

3 years
Language milestones –

asks questions

- Large vocabulary usually understandable even to strangers
- Talk is still somewhat babyish (lots of mistakes)
- Says full name and age
- Has simple conversations
- Tells others what has happened (briefly)
- Asks many questions

- Knows several nursery rhymes to repeat or sing
- Counts by rote to 10 but understands only to 2 or 3
- Matches two or three colours and may know names of some

3 years
Play and behaviour –

toilet trained by day

- Washes and dries hands with supervision
- Toilet trained
- Pulls pants up and down
- Usually dry through the night
- Less tantrums, more cooperative
- Tries to help adult with tasks
- Tries to be tidy

- Detailed make-believe play, inventing people and objects
- Joins in pretend play with others
- Enjoys floor play with toys, alone or with siblings

- Understands sharing
- Beginning to understand the need to wait until later

This page is for you to write on.

Tracking my child's journey

Name: Date:

Age:

Big movements:

Hand movements:

Speech and understanding:

Social behaviour and play:

Comments (e.g. illnesses):

4 years

4 years

Movement milestones -

hops

- Hops and stands on one foot up to five seconds
- Walks and runs up and down stairs without support
- Climbs ladders and trees
- Expert on trike
- Kicks ball forward
- Throws ball overhand
- Can use a bat
- Catches bounced ball most of the time
- Moves forward and backward with agility

4 years

Milestones in hand and finger skills –

draws and paints

- Holds pencil like an adult
- Draws a person with two to four body parts
- Stacks 10 blocks
- Uses scissors
- Draws circles and squares
- Draws recognizable house
- Begins to copy some capital letters
- Eats skillfully with spoon and fork
- Brushes teeth with supervision

4 years

Language milestones –

uses sentences

- Understands the concepts of "same" and "different"
- Names four colours correctly

- Has mastered some basic rules of grammar
- Speaks well in sentences
- Speaks clearly enough for strangers to understand
- Tells long stories
- Always asking questions
- Counts to 20 by rote and counting objects correctly to 5

4 years

Cognitive milestones –

same + different

- Approaches problems from a single point of view
- Begins to have a clearer sense of time – past, present and future
- Follows three-part commands
- Recalls parts of a story
- Understands the concept of same/different
- Engages in pretend play

4 years

Social and emotional milestones –

takes turns & shares

- Interested in new experiences
- Cooperates with other children
- Dramatic pretend games e.g. "Mum" or "Dad" with dressing up
- Increasingly inventive in fantasy play
- Floor games complicated; habits less tidy
- Dresses and undresses (not buttons or ties)
- Likes companionship of other children
- Quarrels with playmates if crossed
- Negotiates solutions to conflicts
- More independent and willful
- Shows sense of humour

- Imagines that many unfamiliar images may be "monsters"
- Views self as a whole person involving body, mind, and feelings
- Often cannot distinguish between fantasy and reality
- Understands taking turns and sharing

This page is for you to write on.

Tracking my child's journey

Name: Date:

Age:

Big movements:

Hand movements:

Speech and understanding:

Social behaviour and play:

Comments (e.g. illnesses):

5 years

5 years
Movement milestones

Stands on one foot 10 seconds

- Active and skillful climbing, swinging and stunts
- Hops, can do forward rolls
- Walks easily along narrow line
- Moves rhythmically to music
- Stands on one foot for ten seconds or longer
- Plays ball games with scoring and rules
- May be able to skip

5 years
Milestones in hand and finger skills

draws triangle

- Good control of pencil
- Copies triangle and other geometric patterns
- Draws person with body
- Prints some letters
- Draws a house with some detail
- Colours pictures, staying inside the lines

- Dresses and undresses without assistance
- Uses fork, spoon, and (sometimes) a table knife well
- Usually cares for own toilet needs

5 years

Language milestones

longer sentences

- Speaks fluently and usually correctly
- Loves to be read stories
- Recalls parts of a stories
- Uses future tense
- Tells others long stories
- Says name and address, age and often birthday
- Enjoys jokes

5 years

Cognitive milestones

knows 4 colours

- Can count ten or more objects

- Correctly names several colors

- Better understands the concept of clock time

- Knows about things used every day in the home (money, food, appliances)

5 years

Social and emotional milestones

chooses friends

- Complex group pretend play

- Dresses and undresses independently

- Understands need for tidiness but needs constant reminders

- Wants to be like friends and to please them

- Comforts playmates when upset

- Aware of gender

- More likely to agree to rules and understands fair play

- Likes to sing, dance, and act

- Shows more independence and may even visit a next-door neighbour alone

- Sometimes demanding, sometimes eagerly cooperative

- Able to distinguish fantasy from reality

Tracking my child's journey

Name: Date:

Age:

Big movements:

Hand movements:

Speech and understanding:

Social behaviour and play:

Comments (e.g. illnesses):

RECOGNISING DELAYS

Generally speaking, if children appear to demonstrate abilities more than 12 months behind in any one area of development, e.g. Speech and Language, it is sensible to seek the opinion of staff at the Child Health Clinic. When making a formal assessment of delays, health care workers will often seek the opinions of others, e.g child care workers and grandparents who may be able to add useful observations of the child's behaviour in different situations.

The hearing-impaired child is likely to be well behind in their speech and language development. The baby who is deaf will shows surprise when a parent appears suddenly beside the cot, not having heard them approach.

The child with specific area delays, such as in speech and language are likely to improve dramatically with a small amount of focused attention provided by the qualified Speech Pathologist.

Delays are commonly found in one or two areas of development only. For example, the child with features of autism is likely to be behind in language but also social skills, including making eye contact. These children will often have poor imaginative play also. By comparison they may have relative strengths in movement and hand skills.

Where delays appear to be over all areas of development, a Global Developmental Delay (GDD) may be suspected. Depending on the extent of the delay, the child often catches up with the right sort of support and guidance for the parents.

Targeted therapy aimed at "catching children up" may not seem important, but as all development follows a step like pattern, a delay can be compounded. One area of delay can begin to affect other areas of development including the child's confidence and self-esteem. This becomes more noticeable as the child mixes with others of their own age.

SUGGESTED ACTIONS

If you pick up that your child may be behind in their milestones, even just one area, it is wise to seek formal assessment. Once your child has had a formal assessment, you will be armed with the knowledge to provide activities and games at home designed to help stimulate their mental and physical growth. Targeted home-based therapy of this kind will assist your child to reach the next vital step in their progress. We want children to learn and to be happy, and this kind of help will ensure they have the best chance of this.

It is my recommendation that you not be tempted to "wait and see". It is now well recognised that early intervention for children with delays is essential. It is the ideal way of ensuring they get the best start in life. Additionally, assessment by an experience professional in child development may simply reassure you that all is well.

N.B. Some services have waiting-lists, so the earlier you seek assistance, the sooner you are likely to be seen. Early intervention at the youngest possible age, allows the child to catch up and be the best they can be.

ACKNOWLEDGEMENTS

During my career as an assessor of children's development, I used many different standardised tools. These were derived primarily from the work of several hard-working professionals across the world. The primary influences include:

Swiss psychologist, Jean Piaget (1896–1980) who was an early pioneer in observing and recording children's developmental progress (by studying his own children), particularly focussing on cognitive stages. His theory has been coined the *developmental stage theory*.

Arnold Gesell (1880 – 1961) was an American psychologist, paediatrician and professor at Yale University. He made remarkable contributions to the fields of child development.

He produced the *Gesell Developmental Schedules* which have been used extensively by Paediatric professionals the world over. Another influencer was the English/Australian Psychologist, **Dr. Ruth Griffiths** OBE (1895 – 1973), who produced detailed scales for the assessment of children. The *Griffiths Mental Development Scales* have been a standard for generations of child health professionals. The Milestones listed in this book represent the average for the age range based on various existing scales and on my own experience. Generally, there is a wide range of "normal". These milestones should only be used as a rough guide. If concerned, please seek advice from your local Child Health Service. The multidisciplinary team assists families to make informed choices about setting developmental goals for their child.

www.ingramcontent.com/pod-product-compliance
Lightning Source LLC
Chambersburg PA
CBHW041213150726
48006CB00016B/2232